The American War of Independence

R. E. Evans

Published in cooperation with Cambridge University Press
Lerner Publications Company, Minneapolis

Editors' Note: In preparing this edition of *The Cambridge Topic Books* for publication, the editors have made only a few minor changes in the original material. In some isolated cases, British spelling and usage were altered in order to avoid possible confusion for our readers. Whenever necessary, information was added to clarify references to people, places, and events in British history. An index was also provided in each volume.

LIBRARY OF CONGRESS CATALOGING IN PUBLICATION DATA

Evans, R. E.
The American War of Independence.

(A Cambridge Topic Book)
Original ed. published under title: The War of American Independence.
Includes index.
SUMMARY: An account of the American War of Independence with particular emphasis on the military conduct of the war.

1. United States—History—Revolution, 1775-1783—Campaigns and battles—Juvenile literature. [1. United States—History—Revolution, 1775-1783—Campaigns and batttles] I. Title.

E230.E92 1977   973.3'3   76-22413
ISBN 0-8225-1201-7

This edition first published 1977 by Lerner Publications Company by permission of Cambridge University Press.

Original edition copyright © 1976 by Cambridge University Press as part of *The Cambridge Introduction to the History of Mankind: Topic Book* under the title *The War of American Independence.*

International Standard Book Number: 0-8225-1201-7
Library of Congress Catalog Card Number: 76-22413

Manufactured in the United States of America.

This edition is available exclusively from:
Lerner Publications Company, 241 First Avenue North, Minneapolis, Minnesota 55401

Contents

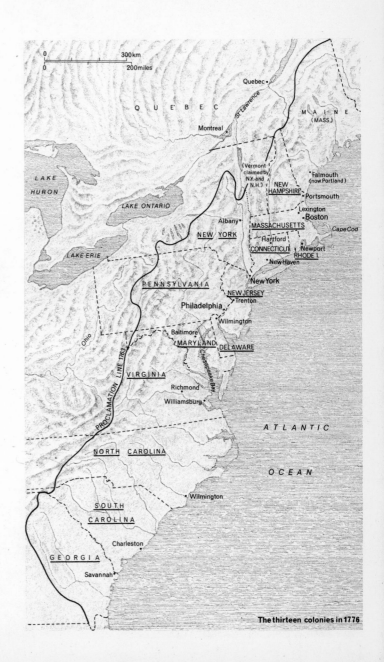

The thirteen colonies in 1776

Introduction

You will know from your own experience that quarrels between members of a family are sometimes very bitter. Although it is often unwise to say that family relationships are similar to those of countries, in the case of the quarrel between Great Britain and her American colonies it does seem at times like a trial of strength between a parent determined to carry on in old accustomed ways and a rapidly growing child ready to stand on its own feet and make its own decisions. The English-born rebel Tom Paine asked in 1776 'Is it the interest of a man to be a boy all his life?' Earlier in the century the Frenchman Jean de Crevecoeur, who lived in America, observed that a European going there 'no sooner breathes our air than he begins to forget his former servitude and dependence . . . and this inspires him with those new thoughts which mark an American'. A mother country which regarded colonies as possessions under its complete control needed to be aware of such feelings.

The English people who settled in North America went there for many different reasons. Some went because they were not allowed to worship in the way they wanted, some went to make their fortunes, and some probably went for adventure. In the early days, the colonists were glad to have the protection of Britain, particularly as France and Spain were also building empires. They accepted a good deal of advice from Britain, and control over what they grew and what they exported from the new country. By the Navigation Acts of the seventeenth century, Britain ruled that colonial goods were to be carried in British ships first to Britain, and then on to other parts of the world, in order to exclude foreign rivals.

The colonists came from many European countries as well as Britain (Sweden, Holland, Germany, to mention only three), and as they increased in number and grew stronger, so they began to find that close supervision from London was sometimes a nuisance. Some colonial merchants made good profits by dodging British trading rules. They did very well for themselves by smuggling, and this meant, of course, that Britain lost money by not being able to handle all the rich colonial trade herself. In the early eighteenth century, the British government under Walpole was prepared to leave things alone, so long as the empire was prosperous, but the question was how long this could last.

You will see that if there was going to be trouble, it would probably be about two things, money and government. There is dispute among historians over how important each of these factors was in bringing about the war, and you might like to think about this.

A colonial farmstead in New York state as painted on a wooden overmantel in 1735.

1 The drift to war

Relations between Britain and her American colonists began to get more complicated from 1740, when war broke out in Europe in which Britain and France were on opposing sides. This meant war between Britain and France in North America too, and the long struggle lasted until 1760 when the British defeated the French at Montreal and drove them from North America. Look at the two maps and you will see the vast territories that were now under British control.

Remember that this victory was a joint British and colonial effort, and that many colonists had fought for it. Try to imagine the thoughts of these men at the time of victory. They had fought well, and had helped to get rid of their old enemy France. Men from different states had co-operated in a new way, and some perhaps wondered if they might now be strong enough to defend themselves without British help. They certainly saw Britain in a different light, and they could never feel quite so dependent again. Now, too, they saw wide open spaces which would satisfy all their dreams for more land. The population was already over two million and there was a shortage of farming land. It must have been a time of pride and excitement about the future.

Think how they felt when their hopes for more land were dashed by the government in Britain. In 1763 there was a serious Indian uprising, which threatened the western frontiers of the colonies, so the British government decided not to allow the colonists to stream across the Allegheny mountains. The Proclamation Act was passed to stop this, and to make sure that expansion would be more gradual and controlled. The Indian rebellion was not completely defeated until 1766, so this seemed a reasonable decision to the British. It did not please the colonists, and this kind of disagreement was the pattern to be repeated in the next twelve years.

As a result of the Seven Years War, Britain's financial position was greatly changed. The wars had been very expensive, and the empire had grown much bigger. The years of

North America, 1756

- ⧄ The thirteen colonies
- ⧄ Other British possessions
- ⠿ French possessions
- ⧅ Spanish possessions

North America, 1763

- ⧄ British possessions
- ⧅ Spanish possessions
- ---- French possessions
- ▬ Proclamation Line of 1763

right: *These were the stamps which had to be fixed on news-papers and legal documents.*

below: *An earlier version of this poster was used to encourage unity in the Seven Years War. It was used in 1765 to rouse opposition to England from all states. Notice that New England is the 'head' of the opposition.*

prosperity had gone, and the attitudes of the Walpole period were out of date. The administration of empire trade had to be tightened up, so that this trade could flourish at the expense of foreign trade. Customs duties all over the empire now had to be rigorously collected. The customs service in America was collecting only £2,000 a year, while the salaries of its officials cost almost £8,000 a year.

The Sugar Act, 1764

The British prime minister Grenville introduced a Sugar Act in 1764 which enforced the collection of the duties on molasses (syrup) which previously had largely been ignored. The amount was reduced, but measures were taken to make sure it was collected. Absentee customs officers were forced back to their posts, and their powers to search for smuggled goods were revived. A special Admiralty Court was set up at Halifax in Nova Scotia to try cases of smuggling and non-payment of duty. The colonists grumbled about these arrangements but reluctantly they paid the duties.

The Stamp Act, 1765

There was more trouble in 1765 over the Stamp Act. Grenville's government decided to leave 10,000 troops to defend the frontiers against Indian attacks, and to protect them from foreign attack. The colonists were expected to pay one third of the total cost of keeping them there. They did not quarrel with the idea that they should pay the £100,000 required, but trouble developed about the way in which the money was to be raised. The British scheme was to impose a stamp duty on newspapers and legal documents, so that just the required amount of money was collected. The colonists proposed that the colonial assemblies should be asked to make a contribution instead, but Grenville thought that this would not produce the money.

People in Britain were heavily taxed, whereas in British eyes the colonists were very lightly taxed and had little ground for complaint. Feelings about the Stamp Act in America and Britain were very different. In Britain the Act passed with little opposition, although one member of parliament did warn of a possible revolt in America. Even the representatives of the colonists in London recommended that it be accepted. But in America it was seen as another measure to make Britain rich at America's expense. There were protests, petitions to the king and Parliament from a congress of nine states which met in New York, and demonstrations and shouts of 'No taxation without representation'. What did the colonists mean by 'No taxation without representation'? They meant that as they did not have M.P.s, or Members of Parliament, to represent them in London, they did not see why English M.P.s should have the right to decide their taxes. You will notice here how questions of government and money are very closely connected. Mobs wrecked the homes of taxmen, and only in Georgia were a few stamps sold.

far right: *A colonial view of the Boston Massacre, showing British troops firing on the defenceless citizens. British cartoons, on the other hand, showed an American mob attacking hard-pressed British soldiers.*

The British Prime Minister, Lord North.

The Stamp Act had to be withdrawn. Grenville, who was prepared to use force against America, had left office, and his successor Rockingham repealed the Stamp Act in 1766. At the same time Parliament passed a Declaratory Act which said that it had the right to pass laws for America. It did not want the American colonists to think they had won any kind of victory. But they had, because they had brought about the end of the Stamp Act.

Townshend duties, 1767

Relations between Britain and the colonists were made worse when Charles Townshend, the Chancellor of the Exchequer in the new Pitt government, extended the financial measures of Grenville. To 'ease this country [Britain] of a considerable burden' he proposed to tax a long list of goods, to pay for the army and the salaries of royal officials in America. A Board of Customs Commissioners was established at Boston to make sure that the duties were collected, and after Townshend's death more of the hated Admiralty Courts were set up at Boston, Philadelphia and Charleston. The colonists' answer was a 'boycott', a refusal to buy British goods. They hoped that this would affect British merchants who would then persuade the government to lift the taxes. In Boston and other towns mobs demonstrated against the customs men, who wrote urgent letters to London asking for protection. General Gage, the British commander, sent troops into Boston in 1768 and under their protection duties were collected, but merchants in England pressed the government to repeal the duties. On 5 March 1770 the government of Lord North repealed all duties except that on tea, but on the same day a mob in Boston attacked British troops who fired back, killing five citizens. As a result of this event, the 'Boston Massacre', British troops were withdrawn, and the soldiers brought to trial. The soldiers accused of firing on the mob were defended by colonial lawyers sympathetic to American feelings, who nevertheless realized that the soldiers had suffered great provocation. By the end of 1770 Boston was quiet again.

'Indiaman going-to in a breeze'.
Painting by Charles Brooking.
Ships of this type were used
in the tea trade.

Worsening relations, 1772–3

The troubled peace was broken again in 1772 when a small British warship, the *Gaspée*, ran aground while searching for smugglers. A group of colonists set fire to the ship, and put the crew ashore. Although the British government offered a reward for information, no one was brought to justice.

In the same year, the citizens of Boston established a Committee of Correspondence which made clear the rights of Americans, and prepared to organize action against Britain. Similar committees were set up throughout New England, and later in all the colonies. They were the means by which public opinion and action was to be organized against Britain.

The Boston Tea Party incident, 1773

Those who have read about the British in India will know that the great East India Company was near to bankruptcy in 1770. To help this private trading company, the British government decided in 1773 to allow it to send its tea direct to America, and not through Britain, in order to increase sales by reducing the price. The tea carried the Townshend duty, but was still cheaper than the tea smuggled in by American merchants. These merchants, who had made good profits from tea, were very angry, and they dressed up as Indians, boarded the first tea ships from India, and threw the chests into the harbour at Boston. There were similar 'tea parties' in Charleston, New York and Annapolis.

Coming at the end of ten years of worsening relations, this was an act of disobedience which the British government could not ignore. It 'took out the big stick' and passed some ferocious measures known as the Punitive Acts (1774) which closed the port of Boston (see map on page 19), demanded repayment in full for the tea, and in the meantime put the colony of Massachusetts under the control of the British military

above: *The 'tea party' in 1773.*

left: *The taxman was the target for citizens who disliked 'paying up'. A lithograph of a painting published in London in 1774.*

right: *The caricature shows Britain forcing the closure of the port of Boston on the reluctant lady who symbolizes America.*

The First Continental Congress meeting in 1774 proclaimed colonial defiance and a readiness to stand up to Britain.

commander. In this way Britain set out to teach the rebellious colonists a lesson.

The colonists, however, did not take all this lying down. They met (all except Georgia) in a congress at Philadelphia in 1774 in a defiant mood. They said that all trade with Britain would stop, and that if force was used against Massachusetts they would all resist. They adjourned, agreeing to meet again in May 1775 if their grievances had not been put right. Lord North's government regarded all this as complete disobedience, and ordered General Gage, the commander at Boston, to seize a store of arms as a precaution. When the troops went to do this, they were opposed by a group of farmers at Lexington, where the first shot in the war was fired. War had started, to the surprise of many Americans and Englishmen.

The Second Continental Congress met in May 1775, and while it prepared for further fighting, continued to proclaim its loyalty to the king, although not to Parliament. It is important to remember that many Americans would remain loyal to Britain, and would fight on the British side throughout. These were the United Empire Loyalists, and many thousands of them went to Canada when the war was over. Also bear in mind that the thirteen colonies were not a united group. They had different systems of government, different religions, very different customs and occupations, and in some there was slave labour, which was not permitted in other states. It would be hard to keep this group together through a period of difficulty. You should also remember that many people in Britain were opposed to the war, and some senior commanders resigned rather than be involved in it. Notice too that very few Americans had any idea of breaking away from Great Britain. The relationship with the mother country was still strong, and some concessions by Britain might well have preserved it for a time. Both in America and Britain there were schemes to preserve the empire by organizing a looser bond between the two countries. The American congressman Joseph Galloway

had in 1774 proposed a Grand Council for America, inferior to the British Parliament but with the right to reject laws passed in London, and his proposal was only narrowly rejected in Congress. In Britain, William Pitt in 1775 suggested that all the unpopular acts should be repealed and that the Continental Congress should look after finance and taxation, under the authority of the British Parliament. The plan was rejected by sixty-one votes to thirty-two. The war was going to remove the possibility of any such settlement.

An American cartoon showing the retreat of Lord Percy's regiment from Lexington. He had come to relieve Smith's troops. The brave American militia chases away the British soldiers, to whom the artist has given donkey's heads.

2 The two sides

Before we look at what happened in the war, we should try to get a picture of the strengths and weaknesses of the two sides in the conflict.

The American side

If the Americans were going to fight against a great power like Britain, the Congress had to set about raising an army. All that the colonists possessed at the outbreak of war were the militia forces raised by each colony. These were intended for local defence and they only served for short periods. They wore a great variety of dress and fought in a way which European soldiers would have thought disorganized. The Congress had therefore to request each colony to raise extra troops, and to collect large sums of money to pay and equip them.

It was important for the Congress to find an efficient commander-in-chief for its Continental Army. There were several candidates, but the two best men for the job were Charles Lee and George Washington. Lee was an experienced soldier, a popular man, but he had been born in England, which raised some doubts about his loyalty. Washington also had considerable military experience, and had fought well in the Seven Years War. He was a very strong and fit man, and these qualities were going to be necessary. He came from the southern state of Virginia, and it was thought that a southerner would have a better chance of uniting the colonists than someone from the north. The personality of Washington was to be of the greatest importance. He was the kind of man that people respect, even if they do not like him much. In spite of many mistakes and disasters his courage and devotion to the cause never faltered. It is hard to imagine that any of the other leaders would have been able to fill Washington's position.

There was much argument about the appointment of Washington's lieutenants. General Ward, who was already besieging Boston, was made second in command, and the ex-

An American officer (left) *and a soldier of the infantry. From drawings made in 1778.*

British soldiers Charles Lee and Horatio Gates were given senior positions.

The infantry was the main strength of Washington's army. The soldiers at first were dressed in a great variety of uniforms because of material shortages. The hunting shirt was used in the early days, but in 1779 the official colour of the Continental Army was made blue.

Cavalry was not to be very important in this war. There was

12

above: *The British took a poor view of the American soldiers, as this caricature shows.*

above: *Tadeusz Kosciusko, who later became Commander-in-Chief of the Polish army.*

left: *French troops. The pictures show the positions for drilling and firing. Notice how three ranks can fire together. From Diderot's Encyclopaedia.*

no heavy cavalry, and the main function of the light cavalry was raiding and finding information. The cavalry was usually badly equipped. There were always shortages of clothing, weapons (carbines, pistols and swords) and above all horses. In spite of this, the cavalry were often useful in the smaller fights.

The colonists had almost no artillery until they captured the important British fort at Ticonderoga in 1775 which had nearly a hundred guns, but as the war went on the Americans received guns from France. Many Negroes fought on the American side, as service and fighting troops, and by August 1778 the Continental Army included 755 Negroes. Throughout the war both sides frequently offered Negroes their freedom from slavery if they would join up.

The greatest weakness of the American army was its lack of technical experts. To make up for this, the Congress had to send recruiters to France to engage skilled officers. They did so by making wild promises of promotion to the soldiers they wanted. Engineers were particularly needed and two of the best known were the Polish Tadeusz Kosciusko who helped with the field fortifications at Saratoga, and Louis Du Portail who later became a French Minister of War. It was their expert knowledge of field defence works which enabled the Americans quickly to master the art of fortification in the field, using soil, wood and sods of grass. There were many other foreigners who passed on their skill and knowledge. Many of these gave themselves noble titles to make themselves more attractive to the Americans, and some of them were very useful. Count Casimir Pulaski raised his own body of troops, and the

TO ALL BRAVE, HEALTHY, ABLE BODIED, AND WELL DISPOSED YOUNG MEN,

IN THIS NEIGHBOURHOOD, WHO HAVE ANY INCLINATION TO JOIN THE TROOPS, NOW RAISING UNDER

GENERAL WASHINGTON,

FOR THE DEFENCE OF THE

LIBERTIES AND INDEPENDENCE OF THE UNITED STATES,

Against the hostile defigns of foreign enemies,

TAKE NOTICE,

An American caricature showing the poor quality of British recruits. It was hard to get soldiers for service in America.

left: *An American recruiting poster which shows American soldiers drilling and loading. Read the small print to see if you would have been persuaded to join up.*

experienced German soldier Kalb fought to the last at the Battle of Camden. More famous than these was Baron von Steuben, a Prussian who wrote the drill book of the American army, and set about turning the Continentals into a disciplined force after 1777.

In 1775, however, the American side did not look very strong. Congress was gathering an army but recruitment was slow. Colonies were reluctant to see their militia troops taken for duty in other states, and men would not readily sign on as regular soldiers. Throughout the struggle, the Continental Army was often to be short of men and money because Congress did not have the power over the colonies to force contributions. In the coming fight the advantage seemed to be with the British.

The British side

The British had a force of 3,500 troops already in north America under the command of General Gage, who had arrived in May 1774. His first opinion was that 1,500 soldiers would be enough to keep order in America, but he was soon sending home messages which said, 'If you think ten thousand men enough, send twenty; if a million is thought enough, give two'. A great deal was possible for a country stronger and wealthier and one with a navy to carry its troops and supplies across the Atlantic Ocean. The navy, too, could blockade American ports and cut off trade and supplies from outside.

Britain took measures to increase her army to a strength of 44,000 men. This was a powerful force, but not as strong as it

14

left: *Smartly turned out British soldiers.*

right: *Britain's Indian allies, who were greatly feared but were never used very effectively.*

seemed when you realize how vast America was, and how a population of over two million was scattered over this vast area. To increase the size of the army still further, Britain hired large numbers of foreign professional soldiers known as mercenaries. Most of these came from small states in Germany. The state which sent most was called Hesse Cassel, and in 1776 a treaty was signed between its ruler and King George III for the hire of 12,000 men, called the Hessian troops. All together some 30,000 Germans fought on the British side, and although only 550 died in battle, nearly one half did not return to Europe. Many died from disease and many deserted. It is worth noticing that the American Declaration of Independence in 1776 complained that the King 'is transporting large armies of foreign mercenaries to compleat the works of death, desolation and tyranny'. But the Congress itself hired many foreigners (as we have already seen) so that the argument is not as convincing as its sounds.

The Indians generally supported the British because the colonists threatened their hunting way of life by cutting down forests and driving them further west. The fierce Indian warriors, however, were never properly organized and directed by the British, and they only troubled the colonists on the western frontiers, and not in the key areas of conflict nearer the coast.

The British had many generals who were experienced and sound, and few expected the Americans to resist for very long. Yet we must remember that the British position had serious weaknesses. Britain was a long way from America and this meant that orders from the government, and supplies for the troops, would take five weeks to cross the Atlantic Ocean. The war was directed from London by a Secretary of State, Lord Germain, and it was difficult for him to keep in touch with the commander on the spot (Gage at first, and then Sir William Howe). Worse still, the forces in Canada were not under the same command as the forces in the colonies. Divided command is usually fatal in war. Furthermore, Britain had few friends in Europe, and France might well take any chance to get revenge for her defeat in the Seven Years War. In that case, Britain would find it very hard to fight a war in several places at the same time.

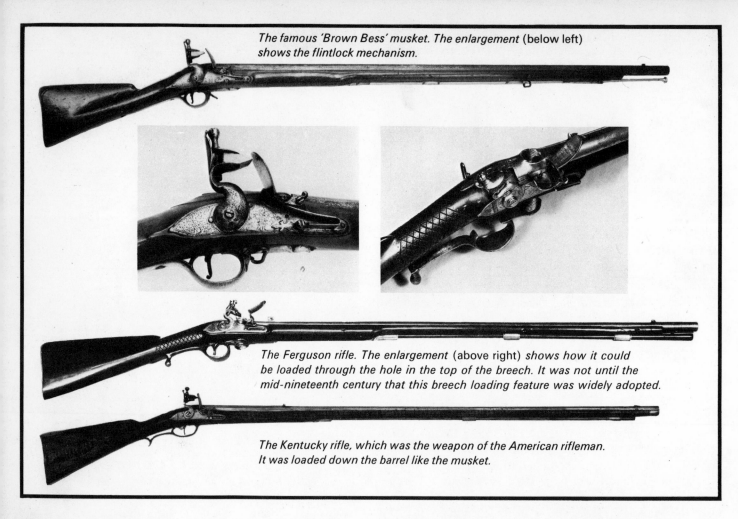

The famous 'Brown Bess' musket. The enlargement (below left) shows the flintlock mechanism.

The Ferguson rifle. The enlargement (above right) shows how it could be loaded through the hole in the top of the breech. It was not until the mid-nineteenth century that this breech loading feature was widely adopted.

The Kentucky rifle, which was the weapon of the American rifleman. It was loaded down the barrel like the musket.

Weapons and tactics

The weapons used by both sides were similar because the colonists were accustomed to British equipment from earlier wars, and the eighteenth century was not a time of great change in weapons.

The main weapon of the infantryman was the flintlock musket. The type in most common use in both armies was the British 'Brown Bess'. This could be fired at a rate of three or four shots a minute, and great efforts were made to train soldiers to fire fast. As the war went on, French muskets were used more and more on the American side. The musket was accurate at about 75 yards (69 metres) and Major George Hanger, an eighteenth-century expert on shooting, said that 'a soldier must be very unfortunate indeed who shall be wounded by a common musket at 150 yards. No man was ever killed at 200 yards . . . by the person who aimed at him.' The musket had a barrel nearly 4 feet (122 cm) long, which made it very much longer than modern rifles. The carbines carried by the cavalry were often shortened muskets, having barrels about 30 inches (77 cm) long.

The American colonists also had companies of riflemen. One writer, describing the rifle, said 'It has grooves within the barrel, and carries a ball with great exactness to great distances'. The

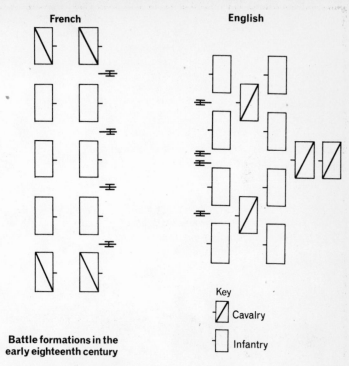

French **English**

Key

◻/ Cavalry

◻ Infantry

Battle formations in the early eighteenth century

rifle had been improved a good deal in America, where life on the frontier was tough and dangerous, and where shooting accuracy often made the difference between life and death. One company of riflemen at this time gave a demonstration of their skill and put all their shots in a 7-inch (18 cm) target at 250 yards (230 metres). The expert Major Hanger confirmed its accuracy. He wrote, 'I am certain that provided an American rifleman was to get a perfect aim at 300 yards at me standing still, he most undoubtedly would hit me'.

Why was this weapon not more widely used? It had two very serious disadvantages. It took a long time to load, and it did not have a bayonet. At a time when battles were decided by rapid fire and bayonet fighting at close quarters, military opinion was against the rifle. Washington and Wayne worried about lack of bayonets, and Major Hanger had to admit that 'Riflemen, as riflemen only, are a very feeble foe'. For these reasons the riflemen had to have the support of regular infantry, and then they could be very effective as snipers.

The British army also had rifles—the Ferguson rifle and the German jäger. Their advantages and disadvantages were similar to the American rifles.

Pistols were carried by the cavalry (and some infantry) and in many ways they were like a miniature Brown Bess musket.

The use of the sword by the infantry was gradually dropped in favour of the bayonet in this war, but for the cavalry the sword was the main weapon. An American cavalry captain said, 'It is by the right use of the sword they are to expect victory'.

Pikes were used by some American troops for defending fortifications and they were often called 'trench spears'. Morgan's company of riflemen in 1777 adopted spears as a defence against horsemen.

The field guns fired iron balls of different weight over varied distances. The most common gun was the six pounder, which was accurate at about 1,500 yards (1,375 metres). If the range was close, the guns fired grape-shot or cannister (small pieces of metal which would inflict heavy losses at close quarters). A gun was fired by putting in a bag of powder and ramming it tight. Then a ball or a bag of grape was pushed in. The vent hole was primed with powder, and a slow-burning fuse was used to light it, producing the explosion in the barrel which sent out the ball or grape-shot.

The usual method of fighting was to draw the infantrymen up into lines two or three deep. The men stood shoulder to shoulder, and each line was close behind the other. From this position, the men advanced towards the enemy. When they were within range (about 75 yards, or 70 metres) they would fire a volley, and then charge to settle the issue with hand-to-hand fighting. When the volley was fired, the men just fired straight ahead in the direction of the enemy, and not at particular targets. Each platoon of twenty to thirty men fired on the word of command, and this made sure the fire crackled up and down the line, and not all at once.

As you can imagine, this kind of fighting resulted in high casualties, and only well-trained, disciplined troops had much chance of success in battle. For this reason the odds favoured

17

right: *Illustrations of artillery from an eighteenth-century encyclopaedia, published in Philadelphia.*

below: *Treatment of a casualty in the eighteenth century. Rough and ready methods of surgery often made the treatment worse than the injury.*

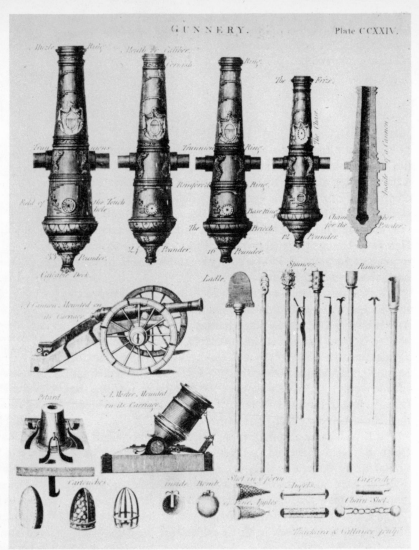

the British when battle occurred, but the colonists did well in small skirmishes and in the guerrilla-type warfare now well-known from Vietnam and many other modern wars.

To get good results discipline was essential, and punishments for offences were very severe. Washington instructed, 'It is the general's express orders, that, if any man attempt to skulk, lie down, or retreat without orders, he be instantly shot down as an example'. And in the British army, General Burgoyne, worried about desertion in 1777, ordered that 'A report of absent men be sent to Head Quarters within one hour after each roll calling, in order that parties of Savages may be immediately sent in pursuit, who have orders to scalp all deserters'. You can see that the commanders were determined to get obedience at all cost, and that this would be a war in which no quarter would be asked for, or given.

3 The colonists alone

The war did not begin well for Britain. British strength was not sufficient for large-scale operations. Although the Americans were ill prepared, they took the initiative at Boston and in Canada.

Action at Boston, 1775–6

British troops very soon found themselves trapped in Boston. Admiral Graves, commanding the naval forces, advised General Gage to occupy the surrounding hills, from which artillery could dominate Boston and its harbour. Gage rejected this advice, preferring to wait until he had stronger forces. In May 1775 reinforcements arrived from England with three new

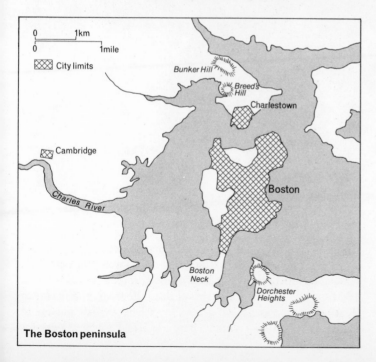

The Boston peninsula

generals, Howe, Clinton and Burgoyne. It was now decided that action should be taken against the 15,000 New England troops besieging them, without waiting for other British troops who were on the way. The plan was to occupy two hills on the Charlestown peninsula, strong points from which Boston could be bombarded. Unfortunately for them, someone (probably the boastful Burgoyne) talked about the plan, and the colonists took counter-measures, occupying the two hills themselves and digging entrenchments.

Now Gage decided on a frontal attack, believing that British regular soldiers and cold steel would soon sweep away the American militia. Success depended on speed, but the British moved slowly, giving the Americans time to prepare. Led by Howe, they made two fierce frontal assaults on Breed's Hill, but were driven back by withering musket fire. With six hundred reinforcements, Howe attacked for a third time, and this time shortage of powder and tiredness ended the American resistance. Burgoyne wrote in a letter that 'Howe's corps ascending the hill in the face of entrenchments' while the town of Charlestown burned was 'one of the greatest scenes of the war'. The British Redcoats swept on to take Bunker Hill, but Howe had lost 40% of his force, over 1,000 men, whereas the colonists had suffered some 400 casualties. (See page 20.)

This action demonstrated the discipline, toughness and bravery of the British troops, but it also showed that militia troops, with little training, could be very effective if in a strong position. It also raised serious doubts about the quality of British generalship, and it indicated that the war in America was going to be hard, expensive in men and materials, and long drawn out. The British government and the king were so dissatisfied that General Gage was recalled, and Howe, who had led the frontal attack, was made commander-in-chief.

By March 1776 it was clear to Howe that the British could not keep a fleet at Boston, nor hold the town. The colonists under Henry Knox had brought, with great difficulty, fifty-nine guns

This painting by Howard Pyle shows the British Redcoats advancing in disciplined lines up Bunker Hill, but was this the best method of attack?

from the recently captured Fort Ticonderoga. The sight of entrenchments and gun batteries on the Dorchester peninsula persuaded Howe to give orders for the evacuation of Boston on 17 March 1776. (No doubt this pleased the Irish inhabitants of Boston, as it was St Patrick's Day.) The British moved to Halifax, where Howe planned his great attack on New York for the summer.

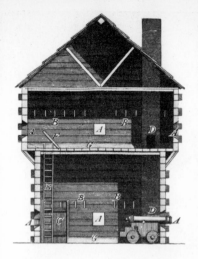

right: Fort Ticonderoga and Lake Champlain. The fort stands in a commanding position. The countryside is still extensively wooded today.

left: Plan of a wooden blockhouse, 1789. These were built as temporary refuges from raiding parties and were easy to defend. They could hold up to a hundred men.

Key to the cross-section, above:
A Port holes for cannon
B Loop holes for muskets
C Door
D Fireplaces
E Ladder
F Trapdoor
G Platform for sleeping on, also used as parapet

The ground floor, right:
A Port holes for cannon
B Fireplace
C Door
D Platforms

The upper story, left:
A Port holes for cannon
B Fireplace
C Trapdoor
D Platform
E Officers' apartment
F Door
G Window
H Holes in the floor for firing on the enemy if they occupy the ground floor

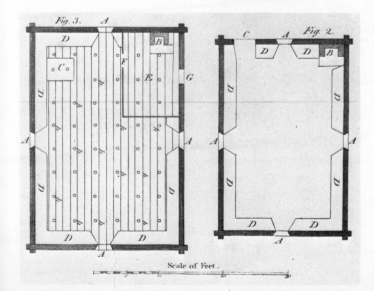

The attack on Canada, 1775–6

While all this was going on, there was action on Lake Champlain and in Canada, which had become British at the end of the Seven Years War. Most of the population of Canada was French, and this led the Americans to think that they might persuade them to support their cause. In fact, British government under General Carleton had been good, and the French Canadians were to remain neutral. However, Carleton had only three regiments to defend Canada, and in 1774 the Americans sent an address to the Canadians suggesting that they join together against the British. No reply was received, so a lawyer named John Brown was sent to find out whether there would be support for an American move against Canada. He sent a favourable report, and troops were raised in Connecticut, under the joint command of Ethan Allan and Benedict Arnold. They surprised the Fort Ticonderoga garrison of forty Redcoats on 10 May 1775, and took the fort without a shot being fired.

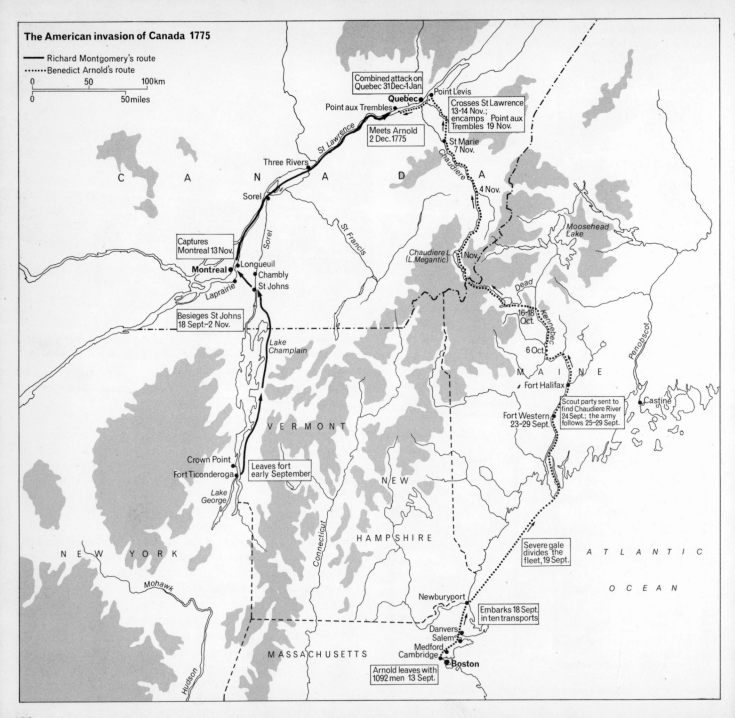

The American invasion of Canada 1775

—— Richard Montgomery's route
········ Benedict Arnold's route

0   50   100km
0   50miles

C   A   N   A   D   A

Combined attack on
Quebec 31Dec-1Jan

Point Levis

Quebec

Point aux Trembles

Crosses St Lawrence
13-14 Nov.;
encamps Point aux
Trembles 19 Nov.

Meets Arnold
2 Dec. 1775

St Marie
7 Nov.

Three Rivers

St Lawrence

4 Nov.

Chaudiere

Moosehead
Lake

Sorel

Chaudiere L.
(L.Megantic)   1 Nov.

Captures
Montreal 13 Nov.

Longueuil

Montreal

Chambly

St Johns

Laprairie

St Francis

Sorel

Dead

Kennebec

16-18
Oct.

Besieges St Johns
18 Sept.-2 Nov.

Lake
Champlain

6 Oct.

M   A   I   N   E

Fort Halifax

Penobscot

Castine

Scout party sent to
find Chaudiere River
24 Sept.; the army
follows 25-29 Sept.

Fort Western
23-29 Sept.

Crown Point

Fort Ticonderoga

Leaves fort
early September

Lake
George

V   E   R   M   O   N   T

N   E   W

Connecticut

H   A   M   P   S   H   I   R   E

A   T   L   A   N   T   I   C

O   C   E   A   N

Severe gale
divides the
fleet, 19 Sept.

N   E   W   Y   O   R   K

Mohawk

Newburyport

Embarks 18 Sept.
in ten transports

Danvers
Salem
Medford
Cambridge

Boston

M   A   S   S   A   C   H   U   S   E   T   T   S

Arnold leaves with
1092 men 13 Sept.

Hudson

22

On the following day, the fort at Crown Point also surrendered. The way was open to Canada, and the colonists now had a large number of field guns captured in Ticonderoga.

A quick move forward might have brought early success, but the Congress sent further addresses to the Canadians before ordering General Philip Schuyler to attack Montreal. He had to recruit troops, and build boats to transport them along the lakes, and this took considerable time. Washington ordered him to move immediately, explaining that this was only one part of a double thrust at Canada. The other attack was to be made on Quebec by Benedict Arnold. Schuyler fell ill and had to hand over command to Richard Montgomery, an energetic ex-British officer. Time had been lost and Carleton had been able to strengthen the defences of the forts covering Montreal. Five hundred Redcoats and a hundred Canadians held Fort St Johns for almost two months against Montgomery. When the fort fell, Carleton was forced to evacuate Montreal, and most of his force was captured as they sailed down river to Quebec, although he himself escaped. Montgomery, with 300 men, went on to join Arnold outside Quebec.

Arnold's force had come along a very difficult route to Quebec. The rivers were fast flowing, which made progress against the current tiring, and bad maps led him to under-estimate the distance and the time it would take. One of Arnold's men described the journey: 'Marched through hideous woods and ravines . . . the company were 10 miles wading deep.' They arrived at Quebec on 10 November 1775. The combined attack led by Montgomery and Arnold (in a snowstorm, with only 1,600 men), was a failure, and Arnold, who had been wounded, settled down with his troops behind fortifications made of snow and ice to besiege the great fortress of Quebec. In the following spring, when the Royal Navy appeared, the remnant of Arnold's force turned for home, having suffered more from the winter than the people inside Quebec. The American force in Montreal was also unable to hold on, and had to withdraw in June 1776. Not much was achieved towards conquering Canada, but British moves against the colonies were now much delayed. Time was gained for American recruitment and training.

Howe's campaign of 1776

In England, there had been much argument in Parliament about the wisdom of war against America. Many opposed it, but the king was determined to bring the American rebels to heel by force if they would not submit. Extra soldiers were sent from home, and from Gibraltar and Minorca. Mercenaries were hired in Germany, and George III even asked Catherine the Great of Russia to lend him some troops. (She refused, acidly.) The British navy in America was put under the

command of Admiral Richard Howe, who with his brother William was given the task of negotiating an American submission at New York, and if this failed, of defeating them there.

By this time, feelings in America were growing even more hostile to Britain. The mood of the people was inflamed by the king's attitude, and by the writings of Tom Paine, who attacked the king in ringing phrases. In a famous pamphlet, of which 500,000 copies were sold, he concluded 'Tis time to part'. On 4 July 1776, the Congress approved the famous Declaration of Independence written by the lawyer Thomas Jefferson. The declaration was a great rallying cry for many colonists, but was also the parting of the ways for those colonists who wanted to remain loyal to the king. Something like 40,000 Loyalists fought for Britain in the war, and earned deep hatred from their fellow countrymen.

The British plan was to concentrate the main force of the battle fleet and 34,000 men against New York, while sending a second force of 4,000 men and ships under General Clinton and Sir Peter Parker to the southern colonies to rouse the Loyalists, and possibly the Creek and Cherokee Indians there. The second force did not achieve much because it arrived too late to help the

left: *The Continental Congress meeting in 1776.*

right: *A statue of the king in the middle of New York was pulled down in the excitement after the Congress's adoption of the Declaration of Independence. The suggestion that the work was done by slaves is without foundation.*

Loyalists, who had already been defeated. Nor was it able to smash the defences of Charleston, South Carolina, which were well organized by General Moultrie. The southern colonies remained under American control for the next three years.

New York was a likely target for the British because its harbour was good, and it was a strongly Loyalist area. The Hudson River could be made a barrier between New England and the other colonies. Washington expected this, and made his headquarters at New York.

The Howe brothers appeared with their mighty fleet and army in July 1776. They tried to negotiate with the Americans by letter, addressing their correspondence to 'George Washington, Esquire'. But General Washington resented being addressed as a private citizen rather than as head of the American army, and he refused to receive the Howes. In any case, all that they had to offer was a pardon for offences in return for surrender. The Americans considered that the British had committed all the offences.

Washington's force was much weaker than Howe's, and the American general made the mistake of thinking that he could defend islands against a stronger military force, plus warships. This was a great chance for Howe to finish off Washington. He landed on Long Island in August, under the cover of a thunderstorm, to attack the Americans there. Washington had chosen a bad position, with no protection on the left for General Putnam's troops, and Howe was able to pin them down, while he led a force around the American flank. The move was successful and Washington found himself forced back, with only the East River behind him, and this was partly controlled by the British fleet. All that was needed was a final assault by Howe, but he suddenly became cautious and settled down to a siege. At night, when the tide was too low for the British fleet to move, Washington took his men across the East River in small fishing boats and escaped (see position 1 on the map). This was one of the most decisive hours in the war.

Washington was then advised by his officers to give up New York and burn it, and retreat to the north to prevent another move by Howe to cut him off, but he did not take their advice. Howe moved slowly, thinking that the defeated Americans would ask for peace. When he crossed the East River in

September at Kips Bay, he had another chance to trap Washington, but again he was too slow. Washington had time to fortify a position on Harlem Heights (see position 2 on the map) and to block the Hudson River with chains and other obstacles. It was over a month before Howe attacked. He went further up the East River to New Rochelle to cut off Washington's army (now much weakened by desertion). But yet again he was too slow, and the Americans slipped out and took up new positions at White Plains (see position 3 on the map). With uncharacteristic speed, Howe turned to capture the two forts named Washington and Lee, and this gave him control of the Hudson River. Washington complained, 'I feel mad, vexed, sick and sorry'.

Washington's force was now very weak, and his spirits were low. He had not fought well, and he had no alternative but to retreat into New Jersey, pursued by General Cornwallis.

Washington moved into Pennsylvania across the Delaware River, and the pursuing British prepared to settle into winter camp. Washington's army was down to 3,000, and his leadership had been discredited. Tom Paine said, 'These are times to try men's souls'. Just as his fortunes were at their lowest, however, Washington re-crossed the Delaware River on Christmas night 1776, to attack Hessian troops at Trenton (see map on page 28). The Germans had been celebrating Christmas, and in forty-five minutes in the early dawn the Americans took 1,000 prisoners for the loss of five men. Washington tried further attacks, but the appearance of Cornwallis and more British troops drove him into winter quarters at Morristown. His troops suffered a long hard winter, and a sergeant in Washington's army wrote, 'At Morristown I was sick of the small pox, and many of our little army died of that disease'.

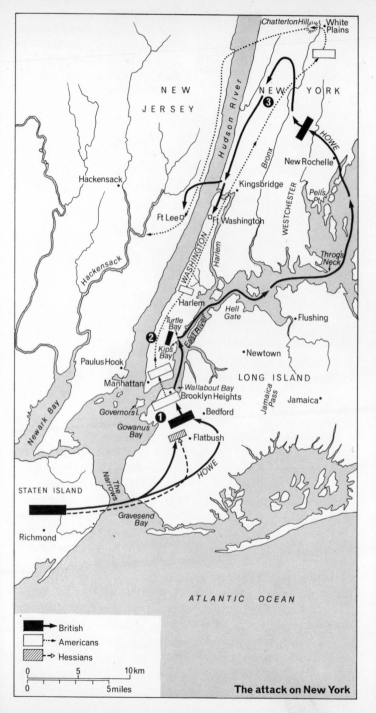

The attack on New York

Key:
- British
- Americans
- Hessians

0 5 10km
0   5miles

The campaign of 1776, which had nearly brought disaster to Washington, finished with a victory which ended the run of British triumphs and gave him hope for better things in 1777. For the British, the year had ended in disappointment. A Colonel Maclean, disgusted at the poor leadership of Howe and the other British Generals, wrote that it was sad that brave men 'should be commanded by such a parcel of old women'.

The campaigns of 1777

During the battle for the forts on the Hudson River, Howe sent home a suggested plan of campaign for the following year. He proposed to send an army up the Hudson River to meet one marching south from Canada, in order to cut off the New England colonies from the rest. A little later, at the time of Trenton, he sent a second suggestion for an invasion of Pennsylvania which might finish the war. Both plans were feasible, but there had to be a clear decision which one to follow. Lord George Germain, the Secretary of State for the Colonies, thought that the first plan needed too many troops, so he instructed Howe to follow the second one. However, 'Gentleman Johnny' Burgoyne, who was in England at the time, persuaded the king and government that the advance of an army from Canada would soon smash the rebellion, and he was given permission to put into operation a plan similar to Howe's first one. In April, Howe sent yet another plan to London, making small route changes to his second plan. Eventually Germain replied, in a letter which took three months to reach Howe, and told him to finish his campaign in Pennsylvania quickly and go to help Burgoyne. Howe received the letter in August, when he was on his way to attack Philadelphia. He knew that he could not get back in time to help Burgoyne, and apparently left him to his fate. British planning was disastrous. The distance between England and America, and the character of the people involved, combined to bring about the worst defeat of the war at Saratoga in 1777.

The Battle of Germantown. There was fierce fighting around this house. Not shown is thick mist which produced great confusion. The picture was painted by Xavier Della Gatta.

Howe and the invasion of Pennsylvania

Washington had suffered a bad winter as a result of food, clothing and medical shortages. Recruitment had been poor. By May 1777, however, he had 9,000 regulars, and the supply position improved as materials poured in from France.

Howe prepared slowly for his expedition to attack Philadelphia, and set sail for Delaware Bay in July. He found that his fleet could not enter the bay in the face of American opposition, and he had to go further south to Chesapeake Bay. He moved slowly to Philadelphia, and now his way was blocked by Washington at Brandywine Creek. Cunningly, Howe moved around the flanks of Washington's lines and won the battle, but typically he failed to follow it up. When he did move again, he outmanoeuvred Washington and captured Philadelphia, but his victory was not conclusive. He risked splitting his forces and put 9,000 men at Germantown to the north, keeping the rest at Philadelphia. Washington decided to attack the force at Germantown, but his ambitious plan failed, mainly because the militia did not attack from the flank. Thick fog added

above: *A street in Philadelphia as shown in a drawing by W. Birch published in 1799. Although it was a big town it looks very rural.*

above right: *Sir William Howe gives notice of a curfew in Philadelphia.*

right: *As this cartoon shows, many people in England thought that Sir William Howe had his feet up doing nothing while Burgoyne was being defeated at Saratoga.*

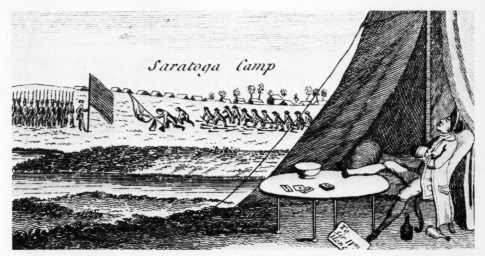

confusion, and some of his men fired on each other. The two armies did not fight again that year.

Howe was now master of Philadelphia, but of little else. He was not welcomed in Pennsylvania, and the celebrations of his troops at civilian expense turned many Americans against Britain. When he received the news of Burgoyne's defeat, Howe sent in his resignation and was replaced in 1778 by Clinton.

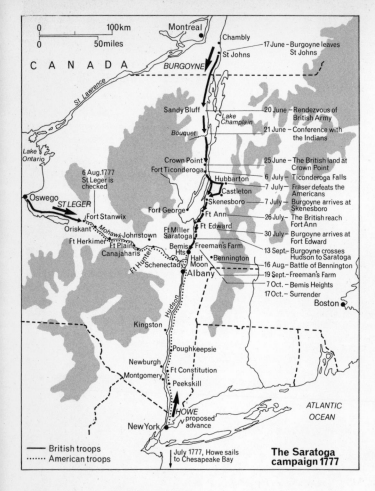

Map labels:

0 100km / 0 50miles

CANADA

Montreal

Chambly — 17 June – Burgoyne leaves St Johns

St Johns

BURGOYNE

St Lawrence

Sandy Bluff — 20 June – Rendezvous of British Army

Lake Champlain

Bouquet — 21 June – Conference with the Indians

Lake Ontario

Crown Point — 25 June – The British land at Crown Point

Fort Ticonderoga — 6 July – Ticonderoga Falls

6 Aug. 1777 St Leger is checked

Hubbarton — 7 July – Fraser defeats the Americans

Castleton

Oswego ST LEGER

Skenesboro — 7 July – Burgoyne arrives at Skenesboro

Fort George

Ft Ann — 26 July – The British reach Fort Ann

Fort Stanwix

Ft Edward — 30 July – Burgoyne arrives at Fort Edward

Oriskant Mohawk Johnstown

Ft Miller Saratoga

Ft Herkimer Ft Plain

Bemis Hts Freeman's Farm — 13 Sept. – Burgoyne crosses Hudson to Saratoga

Canajaharis

Ft Hunter Schenectady

Half Moon •Bennington — 16 Aug. – Battle of Bennington

Albany — 19 Sept. – Freeman's Farm

Hudson — 7 Oct. – Bemis Heights

— 17 Oct. – Surrender

Boston

Kingston

Poughkeepsie

Newburgh

Montgomery Ft Constitution

Peekskill

HOWE proposed advance

New York

ATLANTIC OCEAN

July 1777, Howe sails to Chesapeake Bay

— British troops
...... American troops

The Saratoga campaign 1777

Burgoyne and Saratoga

It was surprising that Burgoyne was given command of the army in Canada. He was junior in rank to Carleton and Clinton. Germain, however, hated Carleton, and would not appoint him, and Burgoyne also had the advantage of powerful relatives who helped his promotion. He was handsome, a good talker, and a popular social figure.

His plan of operation was simple. He would move to Albany from the north, and Colonel Barry St Leger would advance down the Mohawk River to join him there. With 9,500 men and a very large artillery train of 138 guns, Burgoyne set out in late June 1777. The expedition was dangerously short of horses to pull the guns and carts, but he captured Fort Ticonderoga very easily. There were wild celebrations in London when the news of this arrived. Very soon, however, the rough country hindered advance, and made it difficult to bring down vital supplies from Canada. Inexplicably, Burgoyne attempted to go to Albany by a long and difficult route, rather than directly by Lake George. The Americans dug obstacles and blocked creeks, which made things even more difficult for him.

By this time, the American army, which had been retreating before Burgoyne, had picked up more and more men, until it was strong enough to block Burgoyne's further advance. At the same time St Leger's force, which had advanced down the Mohawk River, had been stopped and defeated at Fort Stanwix. Burgoyne would get no assistance from that quarter.

German troops made an attempt to capture cattle and horses at Bennington, but were beaten by the New Hampshire militia under the command of John Stark. Burgoyne lost one tenth of his army in this action. These smaller fights were fiercely contested and resulted in many casualties. Sergeant Lamb of the Ninth Regiment described one of them thus: 'It was a distressing sight to see the wounded men bleeding on the ground, and what made it more so, the rain came pouring down like a deluge upon us.'

General Gates, the 'old midwife' (as Burgoyne called him), now decided to dig in at Bemis Heights and block any move to the south. Burgoyne was determined to fight, and with his army in three columns moved forward. Ferocious fighting occurred at Freeman's Farm, which eventually fell to Burgoyne's men by bayonet attack. Benedict Arnold fought 'like a madman' on this battlefield. A British officer, Lieutenant Digby, described it as 'a dear bought victory . . . as we lost many brave men'.

Burgoyne wished to attack on the next day, but his men were too tired. He waited for three weeks, hoping that a relief force under Clinton would come from New York. Receiving no news of Clinton, he led a strong reconnaissance group to the

American left wing, where he was strongly attacked. He had to fall back into British entrenchments and was hard pressed by Arnold. Burgoyne saw that he could not hold his line, and he withdrew to Saratoga, where General Gates closed in and surrounded him. Burgoyne negotiated surrender terms which would allow his men to return to England on condition they did not fight again, but the Congress refused to agree, and made the British prisoners of war.

The battle of Saratoga was a glorious victory for the Americans and a disaster for the British. General Gates wrote to his wife, 'If old England is not by this lesson taught humility, then she is an obstinate old slut bent upon her ruin'.

Britain was still obstinate, but Saratoga changed what had been a war between herself and a rebellious group of colonies into a world war. The defeat persuaded the European enemies of Britain that this was the time to gain revenge and settle old scores. On 6 February 1778, a treaty was signed between France and the United States promising French assistance in the fight for independence.

Feelings in England were summed up in a verse in the *London Evening Post*:

> Gage nothing did, and went to pot;
> Howe lost one town, another got;
> Clinton was beat, but got a Garter;
> And bouncing Burgoyne caught a Tartar;
> Thus all we gain for millions spent
> Is to be laugh'd at, and repent.

4 A world war

For a long time Americans had looked upon the two Catholic countries of France and Spain as dangerous enemies. Then Congress was so short of money and materials in the early part of the war that it had to overcome its fears and set up a 'Committee for Secret Correspondence' to negotiate with them. France and Spain had no love for Britain and were ready to help. France had lost Canada and other possessions in the Seven Years War, and Spain was anxious to get back Gibraltar and Minorca, lost to Britain in earlier wars. Both countries sent large amounts of money and supplies to the Americans before 1778, and after Saratoga, France was convinced that this was the time to strike down her old enemy. The Spaniards joined in the following year.

To make things even worse for Britain, a quarrel developed with Holland. The Dutch were selling supplies to the Americans and the British attacked their ships in an attempt to stop it. In

Britain is isolated, 1778. In the cartoon, the British cow is having its horns removed by an American, its milk stolen by a Dutchman, a Frenchman and a Spaniard. The British lion is asleep, while a Dutch pug dog runs over it. In the background the Howe brothers are deep in drunken sleep.

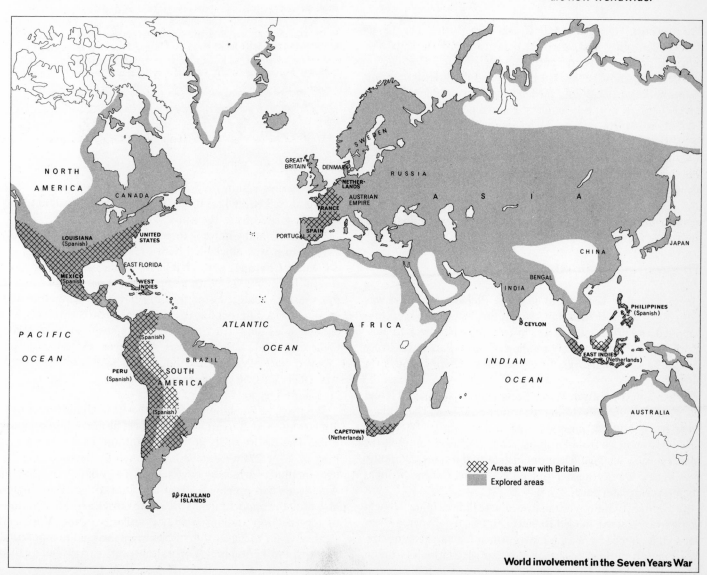

below: *Britain's commitments are now worldwide.*

NORTH AMERICA

CANADA

LOUISIANA (Spanish)

UNITED STATES

EAST FLORIDA

MEXICO (Spanish)

WEST INDIES

PACIFIC OCEAN

(Spanish)

PERU (Spanish)

SOUTH AMERICA

BRAZIL

(Spanish)

FALKLAND ISLANDS

ATLANTIC OCEAN

GREAT BRITAIN

DENMARK

SWEDEN

NETHERLANDS

AUSTRIAN EMPIRE

FRANCE

SPAIN

PORTUGAL

RUSSIA

A S I A

CHINA

JAPAN

BENGAL

INDIA

CEYLON

PHILIPPINES (Spanish)

EAST INDIES (Netherlands)

AFRICA

INDIAN OCEAN

CAPETOWN (Netherlands)

AUSTRALIA

XXXX Areas at war with Britain

Explored areas

World involvement in the Seven Years War

I Benedict Arnold Major General do acknowledge the UNITED STATES of AME-RICA to be Free, Independent and Sovereign States, and declare that the people thereof owe no allegiance or obedience to George the Third, King of Great-Britain; and I renounce, refuse and abjure any allegiance or obedience to him; and I do Swear that I will, to the utmost of my power, support, maintain and defend the said United States against the said King George the Third, his heirs and successors, and his or their abettors, assistants and adherents, and will serve the said United States in the office of Major General which I now hold, with fidelity, according to the best of my skill and understanding. Sworn before me this 30th May 1778 at the Artillery Park Valley Forge

1780 Sweden, Denmark and Russia joined in a League of Armed Neutrality, and closed the Baltic to British warships as a reprisal for British interference with their trade.

Britain was now isolated in Europe and threatened at many points in the world. Would she have the forces and resources to cover them? If not, how could she make best use of what she had? Lord North decided to negotiate with the rebels. He offered to grant all their demands about government and taxation, and more control over their own affairs, but it was the familiar story of doing the right thing too late. The colonists wanted independence. At the same time as he was negotiating for peace, North was sending instructions to the new commander-in-chief General Clinton for the next campaign of the war.

The war in the north, 1778-83

General Clinton was told to evacuate Philadelphia, as it was thought that the British navy would not be able to keep him supplied and protected. He was instructed to pull back to New York, where he was to stay on the defensive. Part of his army should be sent to Georgia to secure the southern colonies for Britain.

Washington's army at Valley Forge (see map on page 27) had been suffering terribly during the winter of 1777-8. The soldiers were badly housed, miserably fed and seriously afflicted by disease. The news from Saratoga, and from France, lifted the men's spirits, while efficient organization of food and supplies by the new Quartermaster-general Nathaniel Greene brought them even greater relief.

In June 1778 Clinton began to evacuate Philadelphia. He sent some troops by sea, but led 10,000 of his best troops across New Jersey, shadowed by Washington's army of much the same size. Washington decided to attack the rear of Clinton's army at Monmouth, but as he was unable to prevent Clinton's escape, this indecisive action only resulted in a fierce argument with Charles Lee. Lee paid for the disagreement with Washington by being dismissed from the army.

No sooner had Clinton's force arrived at New York in July 1778 than it was blockaded by a French fleet under Admiral d'Estaing. Clinton realized that he would have to be much more careful from now on. With a considerable part of his army in the southern states, he could only harass Washington with small raids. A different line of attack was to bribe Americans to change sides, and a lot of money was spent on this. When General Benedict Arnold was won over, Americans were shocked that such a brave soldier should be so easily corrupted. An American Colonel, Alexander Scammel, denounced it as 'Treason! Treason! black as hell!'

What could Washington do now? Although his forces were not strong enough to attack New York, he also could organize raids. The British posts at Stony Point and Paulus Hook (see map on page 27) were raided and taken by bayonet assaults. This method of attack by bayonet was a way of fighting that the Americans had previously been reluctant to use. Washington also took the opportunity to break the power of the Six Nations of the Iroquois Indians who had terrorized New York and Pennsylvania. General Sullivan smashed their military power at Newtown in 1779. Similar operations were carried out against the Indians on the western frontier in the Ohio valley.

The war in the South

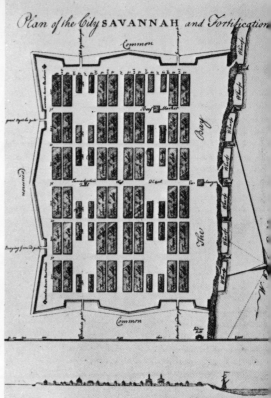

A plan of the city of Savannah showing its fortifications, streets and its shipping facilities.

As you can see, the two sides were evenly matched in the north, and this stalemate suited the Americans better. It was the British who had to *win* the war. They were trying to do this in the south.

The war in the south, 1778-83

Confident that the Loyalists in the south were numerous and anxious to help, the British planned attacks on Savannah in Georgia and Charleston in South Carolina.

In November 1778, Clinton sent Lieutenant Colonel Archibald Campbell with 3,500 men to make an attack on Savannah, with support from a force coming from further south. Camp-

bell won easily, and as a result Georgia was secured for Britain. Campbell wrote of his victory: 'I may venture to say, Sir, that I have ripped one star and one stripe from the Rebel flag of America.' He obviously believed in blowing his own trumpet. In October 1779 a combined American and French attack under General Lincoln and Admiral d'Estaing failed, with heavy losses, to recapture Savannah.

Clinton now determined to make a major effort in the south. He set sail from New York with over 8,000 troops, and in February 1780 he began the siege of Charleston. With the help of the fleet under Admiral Arbuthnot, he was able to capture the port in May, taking 5,000 prisoners and 300 guns. American General Moultrie described Clinton's bombardment: 'It ap-

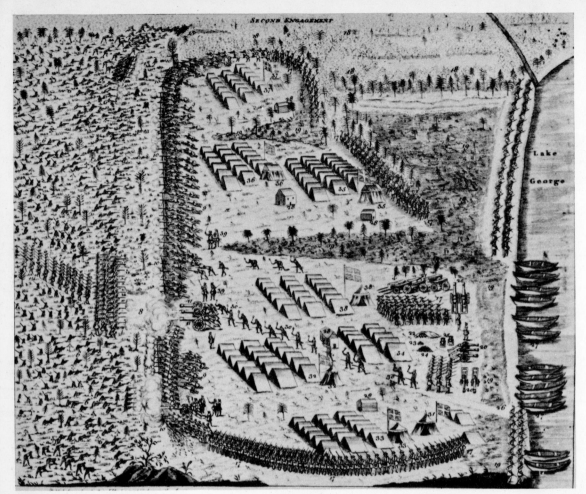

Guerrilla warfare. This engraving from the Seven Years War shows how scattered forces could in broken country attack soldiers in close formation. This was the way British forces in the Southern states were harrassed by guerrilla bands.

peared as if the stars were tumbling down ... cannon balls whizzing and shells hissing continually amongst us; ammunition chests blowing up, great guns bursting and wounded men groaning.' Then news from the north of the arrival of a French fleet and army sent Clinton back to New York. He left Cornwallis and 8,000 men to keep South Carolina for Britain. Many Loyalists took up arms for Britain, and South Carolina seemed as secure as Georgia.

Those who still supported the Congress in these two states now formed guerrilla bands everywhere. They raided, and then vanished, and were extremely difficult to pin down. Their commanders Sumter, Marion and others became expert in this

kind of warfare. General Gates, newly appointed to the south, tried to fight the British in open battle with a force a little bigger than the British, but composed of more militia than professional soldiers. He suffered a shattering defeat at Camden in August 1780. Gates himself fled from the battlefield. His action brought angry comment: 'Was there ever such an instance of a general running away? One hundred and eighty miles in 3½ days! It does admirable credit to the activity of a man at his time of life, but it disgraces the general.' The British victory persuaded Cornwallis to march deeper into Carolina, but he found that the Loyalists there were fewer in number than expected. When he received news that a small force of them had

A print of the Battle of Guilford made in 1810. It is inaccurate in scenic detail, in the way the artillery was used, and in showing dragoons, who were actually held back in reserve— an example of the dangers of accepting all pictures as historically accurate.

been wiped out at King's Mountain by riflemen from Virginia and North Carolina, he retreated to Camden where he was reinforced by 2,500 troops under General Leslie. In 1781, he decided to attack North Carolina.

At this point General Gates was replaced by Nathaniel Greene, and now things went badly for Cornwallis. Greene organized his forces in raiding groups, attacking Cornwallis's supply lines. To combat this, the British general sent a force under Tarleton to trap a raiding group under Daniel Morgan.

Morgan's troops were carefully drawn up at Cowpens, and as Tarleton's men pushed back the centre of the line, Morgan's troops closed in from either side, attacking with bayonets. A near massacre followed. The battle of Cowpens should have made Cornwallis cautious, but he was determined to get revenge. He succeeded in bringing Greene into battle at Guilford Court House in March 1781, where, although he won, he suffered 500 casualties, a large part of his force. In London, Charles James Fox, the politician, acidly commented: 'Another

The Philadelphia *was the kind of home-made warship built by the Americans on Lake Champlain.*

The French admiral, the Comte de Grasse; and the British admiral, Sir Thomas Graves.

such victory could ruin the British Army.' Cornwallis decided to move to Wilmington on the coast, where the British Fleet could protect and supply him. There he prepared for his attack on Virginia.

While Cornwallis was thus occupied, Greene and the guerrilla commanders Marion, Sumter and Pickens rampaged with small raiding parties all over South Carolina and Georgia, attacking British garrisons and Loyalist property. Soon the British were confined to the major ports.

On his way to Virginia, Cornwallis was joined by forces commanded by Benedict Arnold (now on the British side) and Major General Philips. British Commander-in-Chief Clinton failed to send clear instructions to Cornwallis, who unwisely continued to march deeper into Virginia until he came to Yorktown, a small port on the York River off Chesapeake Bay. There he waited for help from Clinton, and protection from the navy.

At this point, we need to examine what had happened to the British navy since the end of the Seven Years War, and its part in the war so far.

The naval side of the war

At the end of the Seven Years War, the British decided to scrap seventy-six ships of the line and build new ones. But money was short and little building was done. The older ships were not properly maintained, and during the American war, the bottom actually dropped out of one English warship! At the same time as the British fleet was running down, the French fleet was being built up to a strength of eighty big ships of the line. The Spaniards were also increasing their fleet, so that the combined fleets of Spain and France were to be much bigger than that of Britain. The Americans themselves were a seafaring people; they built many ships, and their forests had been the most important source of timber for British shipbuilding.

In the first part of the war, the main tasks of the navy were to provide transport and support for the army, to cut off colonial trade and to protect British merchant ships.

In 1775-6 there was fierce naval fighting, as well as land fighting, in the area of Lake Champlain (see page 22). Benedict Arnold, with three hundred carpenters, managed to build an American fleet on the lake. The British went one better and carried the frame of an 180-ton ship from the St. Lawrence River to the Lakes! This gave the British the advantage, but the Americans fought an heroic retreat along the Lakes, and finally burned all their ships.

You may remember that in 1776 and 1777 the fleet supported Howe at New York (see page 24) and at Philadelphia (page 27) without much success. When France entered the war in 1778, and Spain in 1779, the job facing the navy became a nightmare. It had to do all its former tasks, protect colonies in the West Indies and Africa, and the territories of the East India Company in India, and keep Gibraltar supplied when the Spaniards laid siege to it. Most important of all, Britain itself had to be protected from invasion. In 1778 the British Home Fleet had only six fully fitted-out ships! Although this was increased as rapidly as possible, the British were no match for the huge Franco-Spanish invasion fleet of 1779. When this appeared off the southwest coast of Britain, warning bonfires were lit and people were evacuated from the coast. Luckily for the British, a gale damaged the invasion fleet, and this, together with disease amongst the sailors and soldiers, sent the invaders back home.

The West Indies were very important to Britain for their wealth and supplies. The French too had possessions there, and a running fight in that area went on right through the war. The British found it more than they could manage to safeguard the West Indies and properly support the British attack in Georgia and Carolina in 1780-1. It was for this reason that Cornwallis was unsupported at Yorktown in 1781. The fleet which arrived in Chesapeake Bay was not a

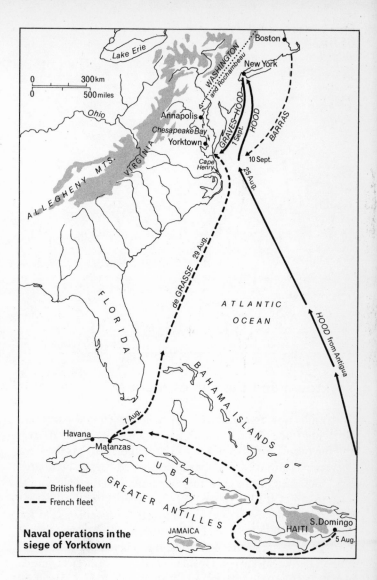

Naval operations in the siege of Yorktown

British one, but one of twenty-eight ships under the French Admiral de Grasse. The British Admiral Rodney had gone home ill, and had sent Admiral Hood with fourteen ships to New York, to join five other ships there. With these nineteen ships, Admiral Graves (commanding in Rodney's absence) hurried to Chesapeake Bay, but failed to dislodge de Grasse and save Cornwallis. The fate of Cornwallis was sealed.

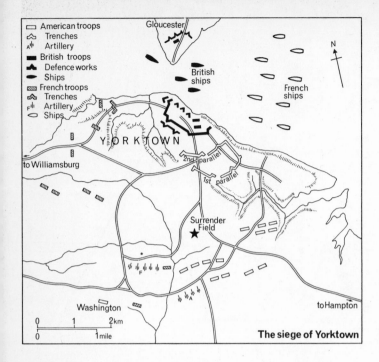

The siege of Yorktown

American troops
Trenches
Artillery
British troops
Defence works
Ships
French troops
Trenches
Artillery
Ships

Gloucester

British ships

French ships

N

YORKTOWN

to Williamsburg

2nd parallel
1st parallel

Surrender Field

Washington

to Hampton

0 1 2km
0 1 mile

Philadelphia celebrates the Yorktown surrender of Cornwallis.

Illumination.

COLONEL TILGHMAN, Aid de Camp to his Excellency General WASHINGTON, having brought official acounts of the SURRENDER of Lord Cornwallis, and the Garrifons of York and Gloucefter, thofe Citizens who chufe to ILLUMINATE on the GLORIOUS OCCASION, will do it this evening at Six, and extinguifh their lights at Nine o'clock.

Decorum and harmony are earneftly recommended to every Citizen, and a general difcountenance to the leaft appearance of riot.

October 24, 1781.

Yorktown and the end of the war

Cornwallis now found himself facing a French and American besieging force on land, a fleet of French ships under Barras, and the twenty-eight ships of de Grasse in the bay. As the siege operations continued, and the American and French bombardment increased, it was clear that surrender was the only course open to him. On 17 October 1781 (four years after the day that Burgoyne had surrendered at Saratoga) Cornwallis asked for terms. Two days later, the British troops marched out of Yorktown to lay down their arms, their bands playing an old tune, 'The World Turned Upside Down'. The American bands played 'Yankee Doodle', an old British melody last played by the British army at Bunker Hill.

There were still two more years of fighting for the British throughout the world, but the general position did not change very much. Gallantly the British saved Gibraltar after a very long siege, but Minorca could not be defended and was lost to Spain. The French snapped up the British West Indian island of St Kitts, as well as other small conquests, and threatened Jamaica. British victory at the Battle of the Saints in 1782

The Loyalist squire M'Fingal is made to suffer for his British sympathies.

George Washington entering New York city in 1783.

removed this danger. In this battle, Rodney tore apart the line of French ships, developing a new style of fighting in the British navy. For Britain, it was the old story again: the right thing was done, but too late to make any difference to the result of the war.

In America, Washington kept together a mutinous, hungry army, and the British fell back on garrison duty while they tried to win the war at sea. All sides were exhausted, and this helped to bring about peace, which was signed in 1783 at the Treaty of Versailles. Britain lost her American colonies, and prepared to evacuate her army. The men left wondering why so many hard-won victories, and so few reverses, had ended with their complete defeat. If British soldiers had suffered much, the Loyalists had suffered more. Those that survived the horrors of war found themselves facing the fury of the victorious Americans. They had the chance to escape to Canada, where they might build a new life, and some 100,000 took this way out. Most preferred to stay at home and hope for the best in the newly independent United States of America.

5 The historians' view of the war

Military historians have thought a great deal about Britain's defeat in the war, and they have put forward many different reasons for it. Some think that the great distances involved, and the geography of America, made victory impossible with British resources. Others emphasize the weakness of British leadership, and others stress the importance of the loss of control of the sea in 1781. Another view is that the strain of a worldwide conflict was probably more than Britain could stand at this time. Which do you think was the most important factor?

As you think about the war, more questions crop up. Would a general like Wolfe have snuffed out American resistance in 1775? Would a naval blockade to strangle America's trade have been more effective than the military methods that Britain tried? Would the Americans have gained their independence without European help? Was there some new element in this struggle which no European military power could crush?

The last question has suggested an interesting line of thought to some historians, who see in this war something very different from the usual European wars of the eighteenth century. They point to several new features:

Civilian militia

In Europe, war was the business of professional soldiers and not of civilians, but in America a civilian militia helped support the professional army. It is difficult to say how effective this militia was. Militia troops did well at Lexington and Concord, at Bunker Hill, at Saratoga and in the campaigns in the south. Yet Washington wrote bitterly in 1776 'If I were called upon to declare upon oath, whether the militia had been the most serviceable, or hurtful upon the whole, I should subscribe to the latter'. Perhaps he would have changed his mind in 1777 after Saratoga, although even in that campaign Stark's militia joined Gates early one morning but left at noon because their term of

service was finished. Fortescue, the great military historian, sums up this discussion by commenting, 'the American militia, a factor which could never be counted on by its friends, but equally could never be ignored by its enemies'. For many years after, all those who hated the idea of professional, standing armies used the American militia as a strong argument for the creation of a different kind of defensive force.

Guerrilla warfare

American civilians also became skilled in guerrilla warfare, and this also had no place in European warfare of that time. The British, like many after them, found it impossible to deal with this kind of fighting. In the twentieth century, similar tactics have made operations in Vietnam, Northern Ireland and Malaysia equally difficult. The British only succeeded in Malaysia because the mass of the population supported them against the guerrilla forces. In the American war only one third of the population supported them.

New weapons

There are the beginnings of technical change, in an age which had seen little or no development in the machinery of war. The improvement in the rifle (invented by Ferguson) allowed the soldier to load through the breech as in the modern rifle, rather than by putting the charge and ball down the barrel. It was another century before this development was widely used. David Bushnell's submarine, in which Sergeant Lee unsuccessfully attacked the warship *Eagle* in New York in 1776, was also to be a weapon of the future. It could submerge, and travel under water, but was difficult to operate. In 1778, Bushnell also used floating incendiary mines to attack the British fleet.

Fighting for freedom

The Americans were fighting partly for the idea of freedom and not, as in European wars in the eighteenth century, for pieces of land. This made them more determined, and there was a new and bitter note in the use of propaganda pamphlets. Prisoners of war were badly treated by both sides. A British officer, Lieutenant Colonel Campbell, described his prison conditions: 'I am lodged in a dungeon 12 or 13 feet square, whose sides are black with the grease and litter of successive criminals'.

Brutality

The fighting was much nastier than anything seen in Europe. The British encouraged the Indians to murder whole communities. The colonial state of New Hampshire, in 1776, paid some Indians money for the scalps of hostile Indians, £70 for a male, £37 10s for women and children. There were cases where Americans skinned Indians to use them for leather. The Hessians had a reputation amongst Americans for their cruelty, particularly in the early campaigns. It is as well that we remember the suffering and the brutality, when so many descriptions of war give us a tidied-up version. All these new features, including the brutality, point the way to future developments in warfare. For this reason alone, it is important for us to study this war and think hard about it. This war also gives us a good opportunity to think about the way history is written. In a recently written booklet, some historians have looked at how this war has been treated in school books in America and in Britain. You will already have noticed at one or two points in this book that there are different versions of the same event, so it will perhaps not surprise you to know that accounts vary greatly. In many American school books the war is presented as a struggle between heroes (colonists) and villains (the British government) and in the account of the fighting, small forces of sharpshooting Americans are brilliantly led by Washington against forces of ill-led British troops, including many brutal German mercenaries. Defeats are left out and victories exaggerated. In the end 'the good guys' triumph, and win their freedom from the oppressive British. In British books the war is often barely mentioned, or the Americans are shown to be a backward set of people, no match for British regulars, but helped to victory by Britain's European enemies. All these are examples of 'bias' in the writing of history. It is natural that every writer has his own way of looking at things, but he should never leave out incidents or facts which do not support his opinions. Look out for this when you read accounts of this war, and when you read about other events in history books. You will see how writers select what they want you to read, so that you will come to a conclusion they support.

Sometimes, too, histories contain half-truths and myths which are more powerful and lasting in the national memory than the truth. There are many stories from American folklore that have found their way into histories of the War of Independence. There is the legend that Frederick the Great sent Washington a sword inscribed 'from the oldest general to the greatest'. There is a story that a Mrs Murray prevented Washington's defeat in 1776 at New York by entertaining Clinton's army for two hours with cakes and wine. The story may be true in part, but the lady could hardly have delayed an army of thousands with her refreshments. Sir John Burgoyne is said to have 'bought' his victory at Ticonderoga in July 1777 by firing silver balls into the fort. And various American heroines, all called 'Molly Pitcher', carried water for the troops and manned guns to support the war. Soon after the First World War there was an inquiry into the use in New York schools of new text books which exposed the myths and attempted to tell the truth. It was described as a '101% American investigation . . .

to preserve the heroic old American history', and the new writing was rejected on the grounds that it tended to 'deaden the patriotic morale of schoolchildren'. In a country of many races, anything which unites and inspires the nation is understandably valued and encouraged, but to be a good historian, you should be on your guard against both bias and myth.

Some facts and figures

Distances

England to America 3,500 miles (5,650 km)
(sailing time 1 month or more)

Length of colonial sea coast of North America 1,500 miles (2,400 km)

New York to Montreal 360 miles (580 km)

New York to Savannah 800 miles (1,300 km)

	BRITAIN	THIRTEEN AMERICAN COLONIES
Population	8 million	2½ million
Armies in 1775	7,000 in America	6,000 (not counting militia
Total number of men used in war	50,000	250,000 (many for short periods)
Loyalists in the British army	8,000	
German mercenaries	29,875	
French troops		5,500
Navies 1775	270 ships	8 small warships
1778	337 ships	French and Spanish ships 358
1783	468 ships	American small raiding ships 3,700
Loyalists	25-30% of the population; about 100,000 left America during the war	

There are no reliable figures available for losses or for expenditure

Portrait gallery
Some important military personalities

American

Notice (1) The many different civilian occupations of the American officers, and how quickly they were given senior appointments. (2) The ups and downs in the careers of so many of them.

General George Washington (1732–99)

Washington was born of a wealthy Virginian family, but his school education finished at fifteen, and he was weak in all areas of learning except mathematics. He trained to become a surveyor, but on his brother's death inherited the family estate. He was made commander of the Virginia militia in 1755, when he was only twenty-three, and in the Seven Years War he fought under the English Generals Braddock and Forbes, helping to drive the French out of the Ohio valley. From 1761 he lived the life of a prosperous planter until the quarrel with England brought him into politics. At the meetings of the Congress in 1774 he pressed for military preparations, always attending the meetings in uniform. Throughout the war he was the driving force behind the American army, and after the war was over, he had great political power and influence, and became the first President of the United States.

General Benedict Arnold (1741–1801)

General in the army, and traitor! Arnold was an enterprising, imaginative soldier, sometimes called 'the whirlwind general', who had been a bookseller, merchant and horse-dealer. He was a very strong man, of restless energy, and this was seen in his exploits against Canada, and General Burgoyne. He quickly made his plans, and believed in suffering the same conditions as

his men. He showed little respect for those brother officers whom he thought incompetent, and was always quarrelling. He was accused of mishandling public money, but was cleared of the charge. In 1779 we find him committing treason, having talks with the British about joining them for money. After the war he settled in Britain, but his past history always followed him and he died a broken man, leaving his family in poverty and debt.

General Horatio Gates (1728–1806)

He was born in England and served in the British army in the Seven Years War. He retired on half pay in 1766, and with the help of Washington settled in Virginia in 1772. Through Washington's influence he was appointed general in June 1775, and

was given command of the army in the Northern Department. After Saratoga his reputation soared, and there were demands for him to be made commander-in-chief. In 1780 he was sent south to save the situation there, but he took on Cornwallis with an inadequate force and was beaten. He fled from the battlefield and was disgraced. Later he was cleared of misconduct and retired, freeing all his slaves in 1786. He was a red-faced man who wore thick spectacles, and he was greatly disliked by many on both sides of the Atlantic.

General Nathaniel Greene (1742–86)

As a boy, Greene was a good student, and went to work in the family iron business. He had a stiff knee which made soldiering difficult when he joined the militia in 1774, but in the next year he was made a general in the Continental Army. He was in the early fighting at Boston, and was made Quartermaster-general in 1778. He was successful in improving the administration and the supply system, but his methods made him enemies. He resigned in August 1780 but was soon back as the commander in the south. Here, as the great historian Fortescue says, his skilful use of his guerrilla troops marked him out as a great commander. He ended the war deep in debt, and died of sunstroke in 1785, just as he had sorted out his tangled affairs.

General Charles Lee (1731–82)

He was an able soldier of fortune who joined the British army in 1747, served in America in the Seven Years War, and was retired on half pay in 1763. He served in the armies of Poland until 1770, when he was sent home ill. In 1773 he went to America, and urged the Americans to make military

Marquis de Lafayette (1757–1834)

He joined the French army in 1771. When war broke out in America, he sympathized with the cause and saw good opportunities for himself in it. Washington liked him, and he was soon made a general, although he was young. His nobility and his great wealth and influence made him very useful

preparations. He was appointed major general in 1775. He was often critical of Washington, who regarded him with suspicion. Lee was captured in 1776, when he submitted a plan to the British telling them how to beat the Americans! He was exchanged for other prisoners in 1778, but soon made himself unpopular by grumbling about other officers and by failing in the Monmouth campaign in 1778. He was suspended for a year, and then dismissed.

Daniel Morgan (1736–1802)

He was the grandson of a Welsh immigrant, and was a farm labourer when he joined Braddock's expedition in 1755. In 1756 he was sentenced to 500 lashes by the British for striking an officer. He went back to farming until the war. He took part in Arnold's expedition, and in 1777 he raised a body of 500 sharpshooters known as 'Morgan's Rangers'. He resigned in 1779 because he was disappointed over promotion, but he came back in 1780 to work well with General Greene and to win a

small but important victory at Cowpens in 1781. He resigned again in February 1781, but returned to fight again before the end of the war.

Two guerrilla commanders

General Thomas Sumter (1734–1832)

He was one of America's greatest guerrilla fighters, leading a group in South Carolina. Known as the 'Gamecock', he was a bold leader, but others found it difficult to work with him. He made the war in the south more vicious by recruiting his men with the promise of plunder taken from Loyalists, and this led to unpopularity, and his retirement in 1781.

Francis Marion (1732–95)

He was a farmer who became a captain in the militia of South Carolina. His nickname of 'Swamp Fox' will tell you that he was another southern guerrilla leader. The great difference between Marion and Sumter was that Marion found it easy to work with Greene, who was commander in the south.

to the Americans. He did not see much action, but spent a great deal of money on the American cause.

Lieutenant-General Comte de Rochambeau (1750–1813)

He was a French nobleman who was appointed commander of the French force

sent to America in 1780. He co-operated with Washington in the Yorktown campaign, and was rewarded with promotion when he returned home.

General Baron von Steuben (1730–94)

He had been a captain in the Prussian army and had served with Frederick the Great in the Seven Years War. He was dismissed for obscure reasons in 1763, but through the French Minister of War he made contact with recruiter Silas Deane, who recommended him to Congress as a 'Lieutenant General in the King of Prussia's service', although in fact he had never risen above captain. He was successful in training the Continental Army, and was appointed inspector general in 1778. At the end of the war, he was rewarded with grants of land, a jewelled sword and a pension. He retired to the township of Steuben in New York state.

British

General John Burgoyne (1722–92)

'Gentleman Johnny' Burgoyne was an extraordinary character. He was a wild gambler, a heavy drinker, an amateur actor, a playwright, and of course a soldier. He had a great sense of humour, and made fun of Gage's leadership at Boston by writing a farce called *The Siege of Boston* which was given many performances. He was convinced that he himself was a great soldier, and went to defeat at Saratoga boasting of his great abilities. After capture, he was allowed to go to England on parole in 1778, and tried to put the blame for his defeat on other people. He broke his word and did not return to America. He spent his remaining years dabbling in politics and writing more plays.

General Henry Clinton (1738–95)

Clinton was a small, podgy figure who had risen to the rank of colonel in the Seven Years War. He was very critical of Howe's leadership and was ready to resign over it in 1776, but was placated by the award of a knighthood. He replaced Howe as commander-in-chief in 1778, and was

unlucky to be made the scapegoat for all the misfortunes that followed.

General Charles Cornwallis (1738–1805)

There is great controversy about Cornwallis. Some see him as the greatest of the British generals in the American War of Independence; others say that his mistakes in the south in 1780–1 lost the war for Britain. He had served in the Seven Years War, and arrived in America in 1776 to join the Clinton attack on Charleston. He was promoted to lieutenant general in 1778, and was given command of the troops in the southern states in 1780. His campaign resulted in the surrender at Yorktown in 1781, and it seems odd that Clinton bore the brunt of the blame for this disaster. Cornwallis was exchanged for another prisoner in 1782, and later became a famous governor general of India.

General Thomas Gage (1719–87)

Gage joined the army about 1740, and served in the War of the Austrian Succession (1740–8) and in the Seven Years War. He was well liked and known as 'Honest Tom'. The American colonists came to respect him as the British commander-in-chief in America after 1763, and he showed great talents as a politician. In the end, however, Gage was hated in America because he was too tough, and criticized in England because he was not tough enough.

Sir William Howe (1729–1814)

Sir William Howe was British commander-in-chief 1775–8. An aristocrat who had entered the army in 1746, he served with distinction in the Seven Years War. He earned high praise from General Wolfe and ended the war with a brilliant record. He

did not want to lead the fight against the colonists, whom he had admired. This and a strong streak of laziness is perhaps responsible for his over-caution and lack of success. He returned home in 1778, and carried on a long argument with Burgoyne about the responsibility for failure.

Lord Richard Howe (1726–99)

Lord Richard Howe was given the naval command in America in 1776, and with his brother attempted to make peace with the colonists. Dissatisfied with the support from London, he resigned in 1778. Late in the war he took a prominent part in the relief of Gibraltar.

Admiral George Brydges Rodney (1719–92)

Rodney was a veteran of the wars of the Austrian Succession and the Seven Years War. He was always in financial trouble and was not solvent until he was made an admiral in 1778. He suffered badly from gout, and bad health interrupted his service in the later part of the American war. He was unable to prevent the defeat of Cornwallis at Yorktown, but won a great victory over the French at the Battle of the Saints in 1782. This embarrassed the government, which had already appointed his successor. To make amends for the slight, the government loaded him with many honours and made him a hero.

Index

Acknowledgments

The author and publisher would like to thank the following for permission to reproduce illustrations:
Cover, Musée de Versailles, clichés des Musées Nationaux; p. 1 (Washington) Independence Hall, Philadelphia; pp. 1 (George III), 47 (Cornwallis, Clinton, Burgoyne), 48 (Gage) W. L. Clements Library, University of Michigan; p. 4 New York State Historical Association, Cooperstown, New York; pp. 7, 9 (Tea Party), 13 (Kosciusko), 38, 46 (Lafayette), 47 (von Steuben), 48 (Howe and Rodney) Mary Evans Picture Library; pp. 7, 29, 32, 40 New York Historical Society; p. 8 (ships) National Maritime Museum, London; pp. 8, 14 (poster) The Bettmann Archive; pp. 9, 10, 11, 14, 21 (blockhouse), 23, 25, 37 British Museum; p. 13 Metropolitan Museum of Art, New York; pp. 13 (French soldiers), 18 (surgery), 35 Cambridge University Library; pp. 15, 16 (Brown Bess), 26 National Army Museum, Chelsea; p. 15 (Indians) Courtauld Institute of Art; p. 16 (Ferguson rifle) Scottish United Services Museum, Edinburgh; p. 16 (Kentucky rifle) Department of the Environment; p. 20 Delaware Art Museum, Delaware, U.S.A.; pp. 21, 31 Fort Ticonderoga Museum; pp. 24, 29 Historical Society of Pennsylvania; p. 28 Valley Forge Historical Association; p. 34 Popperfoto; p. 36 John Carter Brown Library, Brown University; p. 37 Anne S. K. Brown Military Collection, Brown University; pp. 40, 41 Library of Congress; p. 46 (Lee) New York Public Library; p. 46 (Morgan) Yale University Art Gallery; p. 18 (artillery) American Antiquarian Society.
The drawing of the boat on p. 38 is by Graham Humphreys.

Maps by Reg Piggott

cover: *The surrender at Yorktown, October 1781, by Van Blarenberghe. British troops are marching out of Yorktown between rows of French and American soldiers. Some British soldiers are laying down their arms on the ground behind the parading troops. Several men threw down their arms in an attempt to damage them.*

The Cambridge History Library

The Cambridge Introduction to History
Written by Trevor Cairns

PEOPLE BECOME CIVILIZED

THE ROMANS AND THEIR EMPIRE

BARBARIANS, CHRISTIANS, AND MUSLIMS

THE MIDDLE AGES

EUROPE AND THE WORLD

THE BIRTH OF MODERN EUROPE

The Cambridge Topic Books
General Editor Trevor Cairns

THE AMERICAN WAR OF INDEPENDENCE
by R. E. Evans

THE EARLIEST FARMERS AND THE FIRST CITIES
by Charles Higham

THE FIRST SHIPS AROUND THE WORLD
by W. D. Brownlee

HERNAN CORTES: CONQUISTADOR IN MEXICO
by John Wilkes

LIFE IN THE OLD STONE AGE
by Charles Higham

THE MURDER OF ARCHBISHOP THOMAS
by Tom Corfe

THE PYRAMIDS
by John Weeks

THE ROMAN ARMY
by John Wilkes

The Cambridge History Library will be expanded in the future to include additional volumes. Lerner Publications Company is pleased to participate in making this excellent series of books available to a wide audience of readers.

Lerner Publications Company
241 First Avenue North, Minneapolis, Minnesota 55401